Dr. Mephisto

Dr. Mephisto

CHRIS EMERY

Arc
PUBLICATIONS

Published by Arc Publications
Nanholme Mill, Shaw Wood Road
Todmorden, Lancs. OL14 6DA, UK

Design by Tony Ward
Printed at The Arc & Throstle Press Ltd
Nanholme Mill, Todmorden, Lancs.

ISBN 1 900072 67 X

ACKNOWLEDGEMENTS
The author is grateful to the editors of the following publications, in which some of these poems, often in earlier versions, first appeared: *Cambridge Conference of Contemporary Poetry Review*, *Jacket*, *The Poetry Kit*, *Quid*, *Recursive Angel*, *Salt* and *Semtext*.

I would like thank John Kinsella for his encouragement during the writing of this book. Keston Sutherland and Andrea Brady at Barque Press for publishing *The Cutting Room*, where some of these poems first appeared. Thanks also to those who offered support for these poems, both editorial and personal: John Tranter, Richard Caddel and the late Doug Oliver.

The publishers acknowledge financial assistance from Yorkshire Arts Board.

This book is for Jennifer,
Callum and Kirsty

Why, this is hell, nor am I out of it.

Contents

The Pendulum

Mephisto practised his incantations and eye contact,
wiggling in his bonds. His frock coat stained.
His top hat dented. Assistants fussed about the knot.
Then suddenly, *pok! thwack!* the trick came off.
The upturned udder of the stool lay in the mud.
A little bouncing around, not quite a jig,
but a dance I'd say, nonetheless – a shivery foot
the last thing to settle down, like a black tongue.
One brogue fell off, *plonk*. One eye looked a bit tired.
Tick, tock, the raggedy body rocked and pirouetted.
Folk shrugged shoulders, cupped hands
and lit up. No one scratched their arse
or scrubbed a hat to shift an awkward itch.

Mephisto took everything in. He'd studied
regimented goings on like these for donkey's years.
The white air cleared and stilled about his face.
His features went turnip-coloured. Some awkward
gasps reminded him to get a bit of exercise now
and again. One engineer joked about a cold snap.
Another, about making a clean break with it all.
The air smelled of cabbage stalks and diesel. All around,
the audience declined to comment or disperse.

It was depressingly banal. Moleskin coats,
berets and helmets, some neckerchiefs daintily tied
above the glinting imbroglio of eagles' wings
and chevrons; they tootled about in the half-toned,
moon-faced quackery of the side-show. The cold street
turned whiter still, tank tracks glistened
beside the provost marshal. Some picked fluff from
pockets, bored apostles of the mesmerist,
and then checked out the knackered stool again.
The rope. The gibbet. His eyes. His prick.

The Gift

I was there, so I was, Doctor Mephisto incarnate,
flim-flam artist for all the inveterate sinners, kiboshed
for once, but my spell had come right and severed this
waif's artery, the femoral as it happens, and I was breathing,
hoo haa, her hot breath into mine like an old bellows.
Not exactly resuscitating you understand. Anyhow,
her breaths were misspelt novenas of the flesh,
plush organs decked out on the slab, whistling away
towards the ripening shade and ticking shadows.

So there I was, perfidious notion, clearing up
just as the boiling cerulean and fancy, crop-demented
wavering of it all started to cascade. So much care
in the deep stains of purgatory, her quim all shimmer
as the cloud-shadows crossed my old gaffe. My sharp-tailed
boys and those grandiose banisters of flame
descending and descending would it be, blistered
and inconsequential? Asphodel, Astaroth, Asmodeus . . .
their icy gusts tinkling there, the garlic and rape commingled
plains of ice, some animals farting about too, brusque
amid a freshly judged crop. Mephisto's familiars belting off,
each by each a botched grimoire of muddy fur and scarlet.
The air cold as lignite or cadmium and the starry futures
just fissures in the plateau, leaking under a black sun.

See those bitter scallions of old fraternity or comely dreamboats
with their flashy, tar-besotted skins all mission and urgency.
Then the teak-coloured glazes on wilted torsos, the laughs
I'd had frozen there too, *contra mundum*, before my bored
smashings and wastings. Her mitred smile outlasting my gift,
and those heads here, swimming by, or piled like rockeries,
or strewn like cobbles I'd say, yes cobbles I passed over once
in a while, tracing the path back to the absolute
beginning of I don't know when.

The Levitation

"There's no shame in it, it's just a hefty contraption
of wires and boards, some snide magic from Eliphas Levi
and then, *yessir!*" Next thing, I dropped like a leather satchel
on the boards. *Kerplonk!* The whole fabric shifted
and shuddered and one hell of a kerfuffle ensued,
until dust settled on the footlights and I realised
I'd attained the seventh degree of concentration
(once again) or had my head stuck up my arse for a laugh.
"There's nothing to it," I said,
"a few tugs on the old poker and I'm as right as rain,
just give me a minute to set myself down."
Then some joker asked to see the whole thing over.
"I'm bored with the whole shebang. It's no use farming out
miracles if Jansenists like you don't appreciate the task.
Watch With Mother'd be all you could grasp
of magical invocations, no bleeding metaphysics for you."
I pulled my gut in, hoicked up my kecks and took a few steps
towards the wings. "Bollocks to the lot of you," I said.
"Come what may, the puck of your tongue
and the flange of your head will keep you
amused for centuries. All's language to you, no guessing who
fabricated that, more *zoo* than *rue*, Count Ugo-fucking-lino."
Anyways, my tricks would have to wait awhiles,
the pulleys were squeaking and those folk back there
in the *Theatre of Hate* would have no truck
with the scenery of this sad lot.
The whole apparatus was hackneyed mock-Egyptian,
and I guess it was then or thereabouts I realised
the moral fabric of society was a bit of a jamboree.
A fine misleading supper dance of gammy denigration;
and the soulless path I'd taken as my own
through all the sorry acts, was just a right song and dance
of ports, pubs and warehouse nights.
Take that time I'd risen like Horus over the gorgeous
chitterlings of a weathered crowd in Minsk.
I'd rogered the cunts senseless before the curtain dropped.
I was gazing back at my long impervious retinue of shadows,
of burning fields and books, of cobbled paths of muddy skulls,
the balsam of calm in some cell

where snapshots of biddies formed an abattoir of grief,
or that verdigris on kids in the bloated rivers,
when I began to itch once more.
Stiffened in sunlight, my words stuck in my craw
like a viaticum. It was all a load of self-serving
muck and ruin, my time had been and gone,
all that's left was a wincing at the vault's
impeccable maths, the bending goddess
spurned for string theory, no magic in the frippery
of these tired bowels. I lifted one foot up, then the other,
and swooped off for one more shot at
bending the ear of *Amazing Stories*
or shaking up some skanky waif
with my fists full of hair.

Hermes Lives

Just shilly-shallying around the place, I'd whirled and bent
to take a few deft gulps of *Hermes Lives*, an emollient

the ingredients of which I will now impart, imbibe, imbue,
and generally propagate amongst my horny crew.

A wicked syrup of the oesophagus you hurl up entire
down the peachy ruffles of the bog. I reckon the quagmire

of the globe isn't worth a monkey's fuck, a thought which calls
for pepper vodka, except we haven't any and, spells

aside, this cocktail makes for some amusing
calls on the savage constitution, *ho ho!* The recipe is sung

from memory, *mutatis mutandis*, amidst a bad case of the craps,
or the pukka quim of the Caucasus in situ, perhaps.

So I jack down the lot and shift to make another jug.
Feeling creeps into my logarithmic brain as I ladle out each slug:

1 fluid oz of turps substitute, 2 fluid oz of lighter fluid,
1 fluid oz of de-icer, 4 fluid oz of nail varnish, to which add

a slug of cum, a dash of egg-white, and 2 pints
of Jeyes fluid to make a formidable binding for the subtle hints

of Doctor Mephisto's celebrated baccy, a cold infusion
not quite rubbed on the silken thighs of Cuban women

more like collected from the arse-pickings of some mulatto
in the heartlands of Querétaro.

If you fancy a snifter, be sure to dig deep,
there's bugger all left of crying to furnish memory or keep

the spectral vision of the ice sheets fair, all's depth
and recognition in the blank stare of bored ghosts. Enough

of this, enough. This evening's rancid and crepuscular.
The drink can rake the ashes of the muscular

hordes, but that Titian-bright cerulean is just a case of tits
and bums the gods have left and boredom creeps its

way across the bleeding caves towards my bunker,
where giggles flood the dark and lovers hunker

above my blue-white face, a tallow sod in fat-contorted sleep,
that's me, calling up a firmer grip on things, my soul to keep,

my farts to sniff, my glass to fill.
My indolent and fetid days, my wishing days, to kill.

Mephisto Sleeps

All aches and pains, Mephisto slumps below
the fractured breeze blocks. Necrosis waiting for
the chalk lines of the quartermaster. All night
the *blam! blam! blam!* of tiny sulphur potshots
with this gorgeous sniper: a Kalashnikov & messianic grin
& girlfriend in the country, *"Two train rides, four stops
below the pines and vineyards and you're there.
The farm in giddy mud and pigs the size of horses."*
Mephisto hears the monologue and dozes as
he understands the cousins there are wrapped (once more)
in hessian and sleep in clay beside the bloody well.

Mephisto sleeps, taped-up like pimpled poultry.
His body draped in polythene, mumbling incantations.
Four and six, pick up sticks. Three and eight, burn the gate.
His Y-fronts gaping. All porphyria and plasmodium
beside the moaning gunman still. He rubs his eyes with grief
and shudders for some ointment and his old official papers.
Potsherds lie about the floor like tampered gods.
There's wax shapes too, of legs and bellies, hips
and heads with horns and discs between
and smiles like clinkers. Blots of tar
like tiny countries spattered on the lino.
What else, let's see: a BIC pen, Oreos and sputum dish.
Crampons. A bit of scag. Pretty soon the gunman leaves.

A candid shade still bleating on about the grapes
last year and winters that could freeze a man
if he stopped too long to light a fag or take an urgent slash.

Mephisto sleeps. His purple schnozz whistling in the dark.
A few of us observe him as the Magus of Attrition.
He's quite the regal penitent really. His lips
unfastening with cockroaches and lichen.
Outside the roof space is all aerials and washing lines.
A green moon sits on the mosque like an amoeba.
The mandalas of some choppers splutter by as each
casts a beam of light on lean-tos and lock-ups.
The city clicks with jasper neon as the rat-runs prosper.

Mephisto keeps on dreaming of gorgeous prefabs.
He dreams of wires and thorn-forests in the dank
emporium of his breath. He sees the soot-filled mouths.

And then, those notes from church bells charge the air
with ineluctable longing. The roster of each note
a footfall of corpses dancing in the streets, *calloo callay!*
Mephisto tires easily of quadrilles and gavottes,
and all the Moaning Minnies in the Theatre of Hate.
He's wiped out his entourage of shipwrights and chefs
with bowel cancer and Nembutals.
The room smells of Dettol and fish. Mephisto dreams
he's climbing into bed with Louise Brooks.
She's startlingly black & white and really quite lascivious.
All page boy haircut and cupid's bow lips.
His desire's all golems and cabinets, pianos and wicked,
wicked fingers, which climb towards some notes.

The Evocation Speech of Asmoday

I'm here ex nihilo & gorgeous in blabbing death
my sojourn descending and descending in the gutter
my scraggy wings & whatnot adorning a gargantuan
fellah for a spell I'd say & in the Triangle of Art you
have me skedaddled was it backwards set between
executors incinerating all them wretched & discarded
guys just bacon rashers & meaty stuff where devils
or some fervent notion called me from my brisket &
I came & eliminated wind stars the dun corpse O
burning & walking widdershins among the ice crows
& maggots imparting that smidgen of truth was it
balsam or ash in the pentagram O west engineer
bending stubby aye & the smooth beige cleft from anus
to glans & the walnuts of his balls & peepholes
I saw you in aluminium & detergent & reek of boils
smitten I was the tv chundered & I went down &
down to the colic of angels with their quiffs & neon
in alternate gloom & well I don't know I kept going
& you called & evoked & I came to natter there it is
a conflagration of mind in the lies of the desert
cocktails purging don't make me laugh you fuck you
calling from the chancre of your streaming eyes
I see your game in the gaping missile and black verge
of fickle horns & rapine blokes & small stabs at
some lesion & behind it all croziers & muons
those ardent ganglions I could never call my own
perpetually stinking & the ivory ones upside down
in sulphurous waste & scorched breeze blocks, teeth,
hair, leather and incontinence pads, the doorway
steaming as I came through sure enough a smart bomb
whatever do you want of me all I want is Mephisto

Underground

I.

Let me tell you
all my cybernetic gnostic life,
centuries, Kids, I'm telling you,
I've pandered to this stage
& art & conjured broken faces.
Moorgate, Old Street, Angel
Folks, I think it's round about time
you joined me
in the trilling of the damned.
I'm glad to be of help here
as you choose the righteous path
through old infernal nocturnes
& my Rolodex of venal souls.
Step up for one more
jaunt among mindless sods
under *Mornington Cres.*
O beautiful & scurrilous whores
of la la la perdition
you're stuck for choice,
homunculi from
Edgware, Burnt Oak, Colindale
just shed your chains & glimpse
my crooked frame above the naphtha.
Goddam, goddam,
just take my hand
& let me desecrate your hopes & dreams.
The city's plumage once discarded's
just an antiseptic wind
all tainted with that rinse
of fact, the denizens just guff & tarts
still pouncing on my lieder.
You know, I've rinsed my eyes
a thousand times on
showerheads, train stops,
the dusted trench & limbs
& all such rancorous congestion,
so take a swig of this

immaculate febrifuge
Pilgrim, the tracks have ended
& I'm sharing out oblivion,
a blessing to be sure.
So jump right in to mix and match
each penetrating shade,
a ticklish choice I know
amongst the tanning hides below,
we're all a touch
oblivious & shining for a lonely fuck.
I guess you'll come to see me
as your original
& peckish wretch,
so look me in the eye
for I'm not asking much just now –
a look-see and a promise
if you've got the gumption
to take me at my word
just step right up and kiss both cheeks –
X X, your respite's due,
your old mechanical
& rancid luck will find
a putrid husband in
the quelling quelling ash.

2.

I have my cabinet stuffed
with hoary souls
I have my burning veldts
back here old son, just
pay the price and let me
ruin you for fun,
as if it matters.
It's just a little theatre as if,
to give this credence, let's say
the very flames of hell
are just a poet's feckless
piss away, so come and take a peek
Holborn, Goodge Street, Warren Street
the Euminedes are fluffers
in the spark-lit dank ephemera,
all bending to the task
as I take you through each blow
(though you don't know your arse
from your elbow).
Call me Horus or Old Perfidy hisself
for all it takes is piebald ears
a rupture of the veil, a hurdy-gurdy
& antic amp below the escalator
Highgate, Archway, Tufnell Park
the tinnitus of swanky crowds
& years of meagre living like a stain,
a bleb inside the temple & you're there
beside boiling entrances,
steel banisters & lemon tiles
& lime walls descending
ah yes below the far-off slinky Thames,
that bloated water
dawdling in amber curls
like a thought in some ruminant
organ of desire. But here
below it's all a game of winds.
In case you fancy some of this
just take your time &
banish from your mind
all thoughts of marbled flanks

where you might dip your wick.
Just step into the carriage,
this gorgeous cicatrice of tunnels
all arteries & chthonic stink,
a journey of erasures & declensions.
Yes, all you can muster's no more than
a weary genuflection in my tepid piss.
I know that I'm an intemperate
& florid geezer goading
each by each in this forsaken
city of all chilblains & distemper,
but take a swig of this & I'll
bless you with a thousand days
of indolence and care,
indeed, ta ta, just leave your soul
for rancid dust, adieu old chum,
a tryst for rancid rancid rancid dust
Tooting Broadway, Tooting Bec
the tainted twig is bristling here,
my brightening and my Albion.

The Flight

Unbound on cross-town streets,
Mephisto ponders. He rides
the puerile undertow
and pantomime of fact. All night
he's ghosting in the astral glare,
his body just a fleshy scurf,
well-oiled and bony in the attic.
His pencilled eyebrows bare twigs
against a diesel snowscape.
The same old tonguing neighbourhoods
and water tanks below
the darting gannet that's his life. *A day and then*
a day at times his face is just
the moon scudding over skylights
where plaintive mothers strangle men
in sickle shadows and whingeing
traffic in the good night throngs
beneath a contaminated hump.
He's multitudinous and free,
quite kinky too although
a soulless huckster dressed
right now as if a prophet
in seersucker three-piece
and crimson cravat. Always the sharp
bequeather annulling and annulling
the salty breath and vanity
in broken beds. His dream gills
working the air like a tench.
He's really just a lewd admirer,
whistling through epistles on the sidewalk.
His knocking tears all things to no one.
His flight all eyes and mouths.
And in the cracking trip of ruin
he's just an absolute slut for
all the downtown condominiums,
the belting and erotic damned,
a fading mattress for that matter,
all urban meniscus and mandibles
flickering as he beams

alone in staring tremors. *A day*
and then he mimes a broken
sound-track coalescing
with the crackelure
in glass and candid girly
signage. Watching (*a day and then*)
as each sight saturates
below chrome skies and dawns,
like weeping vulvae
rectifying acts
in the worthlessness of art.
A day and then a day.
And then a day, all said and done.

The Burial

My mouth full of ashes while they herd us
to the edge, a quick tootle about and one last
shufti of greens and blues, the dusty whin,
the wispy cirrus, before we line up
facing the tree-line. No sporting chance,
just a spurious and mechanical episode
no golem would deign to call upon,
except I was there. Everything rinky-dink
and badly orchestrated. Still, I shat myself
just the same, with my honest affection
for secular endings. "*All covered in talc*"
I thought, casting a glance at the truckloads
in my hermetic trench. But it was just
the quicklime, spadefuls billowing
like dank swathes from a thurifer.
I guess we'll all crawl in ghostly formation
towards some stagnant Baltic mind,
a dissipating haul – a snake of limbs,
I imagine, never getting a shot
at measuring up to the blow by blow account
of the cardinals. Each show was a sell out.
I could smell the tractor chundering close by
as I was delving into memories
of farms and headscarves, carts and bridges,
one hand over my old todger or gathering
an errant lock, a smell of dust burning
on the valves, bizarrely, as my act began.
Rat-a-tat-tat the bolts were ratcheting.
Some more tumbling and fleshy blows
below dour weather and young corporals
with bad teeth. The sentries bored and stood
there looking like piffi, waiting for home time.
The soil so cold on my cheeks I huddled
corpses for a smidgen of warmth
and smelt the sulphur from the carbines.
My ribs cracking under boots as our wounds
started yammering and yammering
for short endings and bungled eternity.
Next thing I was cramming handfuls

of soil into my gob to stop me blabbing
of my endless survival,
hunkering down for centuries
in callous shreds and gathered bones.
So far so good. All's well with my interring
set below the fabulous weight and
crust of nations. First off, my eyes
burst, my hairy thoughts glistened
in my neighbours' juices. It was all antiseptic
roots and soot below outhouses
and goods yards. "Wake up, wake up," I kept
mumbling, as seasons passed and skies
coalesced as I lay in the stinking dark
and history's muddy inches.
There was quite a racket as industries
perfected new instrumentation
to measure the indomitable tribes above.
Pretty soon I was happy to unveil
the skelfs of my legs, my hatchet-face,
my lungs like canisters of peat,
and my pelt plush with dandified
worms, my gob this tired satchel.
I had returned; my old tectonic self again,
shattered among the gormless webs
and blood-wet entertainment.

The End

My ending up like Vesalius
it seems, auditing what looks
raw, shored up and inoculated,
dying for a hit as I come
to a halt freeze-framed
below the east side slums
with their little whiff
and puddled ground,
their steel night tingling with
gorgeous wreckage.
Those concrete genuflections,
my old zones still multitudinous
on the blackbird's field of souls.
My local dominatrix squats
to contemplate dimpled vertebrae
with eyes just slits above
a burning ciggy.
So I'm murmuring
betrayals in the sodium night
calming our nerves, so to speak,
of watchful demons and liquid panic,
so swanky I've regaled
myself not to mention
the running walls, the cabbage field,
the clanking stove pipes,
and doling out such unconsidered
rapture in my mingy arse.
Just gadding about with this
angling for the grave.
A lover surging in the vigorous
mechanics of the soil. It's true,
you'll come to know
all beauty is butchery.

Sebastião

Sebastião, when I cast my eyes across the mine,
across the makeshift ladders & yokes & buckets of slop
descending in the whole inarticulate back-breaking avenue
of my life, the quarter million flensing limbs
of running sores & sweat, the quarter million litres of mud,
the spiralling circles of my crawling brothers in the mud,
I want to tell you how it is among the dead.
The crow's feet around my eyes have set in ridges
like a desert peppered with rain and wind during the dry spell,
that cracks under the strain as the baked land
giddily splits to drink its fill & the winds tousle
the sage brush as the drops sink in the dust like freckles
on a mulatto. I can see shining teeth in the mud
of my dreams, faces weathered with the earth's last sighs,
enraptured there, bleeding ourselves dry for this mud life,
sinking into the orange washed-up belching land.
Or maybe sliding into the undulating banners
of the mine's walls to be disgraced in the admission
of the nameless torrents. My eyes are grey, my face is grey,
even my prick is grey when I take a piss.
Sebastião, my hopes are mud beneath the blankets
and torpor of the papaya trees.
Sebastião, I'm naked with ten thousand others,
a hundred thousand, slogging it out in the mud like crabs.
It smells like a crab shell here, except the damp keeps things
sweeter & more keen. The sea is less blind than this pit,
its storms are quieter but we're drowning here, Sebastião,
just the same. I can see my brothers glossy in the rains
or caked dry as the riverbed last year when the sun baked
us rust bright like the tractors left a season with no cover.
We have endured such travesties in the mine
yet again & again when I taste my sour bread
all I notice is the crevices in my hands & feet.
The mud has crept into me like the long moon's
seething wastes & solace in the river's curve and burden
before the floods. Even my bones are mud,
white mud crumbling beneath the tides of my skin,
its ripples & ruptures as I struggle to make my way
from the lowest circle to the thousand foot,

grape-dark lip of the mine. If I slip
my brothers cannot grip my arm. If I fall,
my brothers cannot dig me from the furrows.
I have served my time twice over & the penalties
of this life are nothing to me now.
Sebastião, my riches are nothing
but the beauty of damnation.
When you come here, watch for me,
I'll raise my arm to mark the way.
My tongue all mud, my speech
will pour you into threnody.

Köpfe

the butchers' heads are sleeping under fished-out light
Mephisto quite shambolic beside the verdigris of frozen mugs
the muted gnawing from our mustachioed patresfamilias

waist deep among darling teeth the goatees in pert folds
quite comfy combing the oily hairdos among each smashing dad
(asbestos dust slow in the culvert once again)

all the interfering vistas tuning in to Mephisto's bones
a racket dimmer than before weaker than before voices
crackling like bacon on winter streets transmitting

exhausted nights and guzzling at the party fringes
Mephisto taps his cane and farts beside such notions
bored with the circuitous putsch the absolutely naked

torpor where mouths divvy up miracles for the people
each ravenous head purporting new customs for hygiene
purloined gossip in each furlough's night-song and cold wires

the echoes beyond cubicles and bloody senators
it's all a case of balding scalps and eyes back here
winsome gazing under gorgeous beams of light

umber mountains cobalt mountains black mountains
each clarifying brow above angled cheeks still cute alas
harping on about allegiances and the patina of empty shoes

Mephisto's Pockets

Some kronor.
A pack of cards.
Two snails with the faces
of Goebbels and Stalin.
A child's wand for culture.
Seven elastic bands.
One paperclip (uncoiled).
Several dozen
handkerchiefs,
shot silk, very red.
A glass ball all scratched.
A small doll
peppered with age
blinking in the dark.
A porcelain skull
(Mexican in origin)
grinning inanely,
with selenite eyeballs.
Some grey fluff.
A tram ticket
to *Kitty's Catholic*
Emporium.
Encapsulated ausweis.
Six teeth – one gold.
A grimoire, its starry
pages yellowing.
And forty-nine devils,
vicious, pink
and ludicrously
small.

The Moment

Blam, blam, blam! Something like that.
The sound of a clapperboard
or a trapdoor slamming, *crack!*
Once only to be honest. He took me by
the seat of my pants and flipped
me round. *Jeezus!* The hollow sun
dunked in brine.
Every bleedin' time the shots rang out
indolence bred rapture –
excess, erection, Thermidor –
no matter else for sure
which sizzles here and patterning
of the exterminator
that was rich
me asking for it though some shag-pot
half-inched it
led me up the garden path *talooralay*.
All that hope against hope shite.
I lay curmudgeonly in mute light
and bric-à-brac.
A bit of a risk you'd think,
but magic had gone out of the occasion.
No staying power although I resumed,
no sooner raked my hips
and dropped my pants
than the same incantations
began to swell like a busted gut,
except the moment gone,
the moment gone,
the moment dead and gone.

The Scourge

The besieged city
upside down
leavening its
bed of nails
broken teeth
investitures
of crimson lips,
quandary
of each
and every
glance above
such gilded sweat
on the elephantine
globe
that is Mephisto's
lumpy arse.
Him piping up
"They're coming now.
They're coming,"
as the fiscal
tune limbers up.
"Tut tut," they say
"a vandal
and a ruddy
scourge,
a ruddy scourge
to boot."

The Hippogriff

A fabulous and dippy sight, clip-clopping about
though utterly shagged as the convex neutral staring came
to a halt, the crowds resonant with all that come-as-you-are
shite and mullahs stung with orchitis waving banners
and screaming as the first bombs went off and the kids
began beating their chests for desultory executions,
the whole caboodle nothing more than a ram raid,
a teensy-weensy ballad and a half of numbing celebration.
Anyhow, *clip clop, clip clop,* down the boulevard,
Mephisto doffing his cap, Mephisto teasing the bit
between the beak and umming and ahing about
the filly that bred this fine heptathlete. *Sheesh!*
There you have it, all in one, a fine beast grazing
the winter streets, the sidewalk purple below sodium
signs and winking windows, without so much as
a by-your-leave when suddenly the wings a-flutter
and legs akimbo the knackered ottoman of its flanks
gave way in the dust, a few sedans lingering
to watch by the drugstore. Mephisto ferreting
about in the gutter searching for one last
indefinable shape, a pattern to dump
the whole divining mucus into and spill
the world's lavender guts upon the spliced
notion of the eighth correlation – that slow sigil
paraded on the very arse of the last heifer
on the planet, a total fuck up and extracted
from the argot of a thousand tinkling pimps.
You have your portents. Take heed and wash
your feet in urine; make this last week's bread
with powdered mandrake, beetle dust and menstrual
blood from eighteen nubile lauded pigs.

The Crucifixion

Surfing as I'd known
because the kerfuffle
I'd caused by steppin in
here to confine mysel
to vinegar and shoelaces was fine
I'd taken mysel off
to the dun tanks long afore
those half-fish scaly things
sommat in that I guess dancin
thet procession all fluke
an jes urbane enough
in the muted tones so I gather
for Zanzibar or some such extravaganza
and that perfumed vertiginous whoring
oh yeah I skedaddled
all tonsils and no fillip
most queer
is all
jes eat me
for I fume
no docket intended
I int kiddin here
either
[exeunt]

Mephisto Sweeps the Desert

"Though I is an old ham in particular there's no ripeness in these clutching paws, swanky though they is. I'm telling you I is an ideal grunt and in gliding dump my load with some precision then back up to some peroxide shunting with my universal distillates, that's some kinda ritual, you understand. It's true I is inverted most times. Refining the pipeline which has dwindled me somewhat I guess also. Excepting I's undervalued here like when refracted planes below, geed up above the console, I'm meagre on the skimpy dustbowl, veering there perplexingly. So my shadows're all a swirl and I'm doing stuff, it is all going smoothly, though I cannot help myself in tearing as such. Obediah was foxy, at the same time it went real fine for me too, just screens boxing and deepening each caper. We were well into it. Ripples so gold soft I came and wept into myself. Ripples quite blue-shadowed and richly birling as I scooted. It's a goddam beach I tell you, Son! Hotter'n hell too. I crept for forty nights and we still mention stuff relating in cold dust upon a Saturday evening though I ain't reeking of fear is all, it's just pertaining to the washed out moxie of it. Shot to blazes I was. I meant each pile of shit though, uh huh. No kidding, we scraped through by the seat of our pants. And of that other stuff you alluded to? Friend, I don't recollect."

Mephisto Redivivus

Innocuous flapping & idling can make a difference
to sinning as dogs' homes blister in umpteen
housing units dearth settles Falstaff congealed upon
makeshift primary sentences blabbing & beleaguered
infanticides toy with notions of the swung joy
money is just a bag of wrinkles until snapping in
to place yanking the coy auditors you elope in ad-filled
turds though quite peaky to be here sensitised & demure
among coquettish webby nudes & next regain
composure in impish weevil tavernas & buttered
pikelets are all a bit of an oojah not quite pimpled
with industry you see although Copernican rapture is
utterly choosy in this especially when confused with what
kamikaze amalgam forgoes I'd rather go for pedigree myself
though far be it from me to indicate positive actions in
making claims of this kind whippersnappers almost always
catch the goats of justice and earnest kinship where the
fusty nuns discard lewd mica & the dew of each is
a shambling fascination with cordite & pampered leather
a little whiffy & a little burgled at the edges
indicating piquant class elation where the lumpy monsters
pass their positronic offsping from canal to fulsome
patronage measure that there are no causal opposites in
bantering & it's quite wrong to presuppose losses when
having a turn of this kind even more so the fashion for
quibbling immolation quite funky & sparky where one can
attend such devices but all through the worst of it the
withering mice of dust met with honoraria met with
indescribably pimply & vulgar prospect & proper sewage
& a right stew till it all came through in the end
mark my sinew Old Stones the grey broth of perspex is far
from brewing here a cordless flight is of all earth's
gandering emulsion just so tara for now I'm scunner
with my orgone pump & off for gunning baba

Mephisto Deals the Tarot

afar I see a small ritual & a void pertaining
to little else for some purpose fashioned I think
to squeeze wild suns in the dun breath *whoosh*
a wadge of light the sulphur clearing a path
the Pilgrims upon which yes the simple path
you will endure some disregard for a messiah
a vehicle of pleasure irate in the spitoon

four of cups you are a proper residuum
indomitable satin yes a caress the primum
mobile scratching the plasterwork that's clear
a flailing gibbon much mooted here & co
a yoke maybe tucked up and absconding
in the soft car golgotha perched above
potentates glib in each velveteen bazaar

or instilling argent knives perhaps instilling
auxiliary love for nil cracking as it holds
up on the spike so sorry the dead skin that
covers it so it comes off in that crowded place
up conquering the bell the fishes jittery
Astaroth flashing a little movingly yes
coinage limp among the grooming sutures

three of swords a tunic in tatters of this world
have it your way rummaging inside
no more reason against regress in pearls
a feature there of baking of possible light
tunes in all to the lavish burn of good mostly
history's yells tiptoe on the left I see
each thing up close & then some ways off again

The Prayer

I've longed to be a measly number
cared you might say to be strewn aside
a stain it is a blessing to be wasted
so screwed down are things pondering
and bearing no confusion in itinerant value
shirking the plural rivers that are the talisman
it is no tale to be erased in the flame
an absent one & not named in the chasm
ashes I guess and I would thank you for it
below the tallow aisles a product I'd say
low in price shorn of use and debunked
free maybe a ruined one currying favour
with a fat zero so Kid will you join me there
somewheres down the line a soul elided
O perpendicular or certainly rent among vetch
tidily gunked up within a yard or two of stuff
of illness some disquiet too it is a small thing
maybe to ask to be forgotten no papers
no care and rubbished in the main
O vac vac vacuo rescinded in low fields
it seems so resilient to be suffered
among tawdry hemp and breeze blocks
it is a cursed thing to be attended to
to be so full a bursting there isn't much
just take the side of each warehouse here
their corrugated plates and strata a calm prefab
quite meandering across a scuzzy site
poxy houses fenced off almost finished
it is the steel I am truly weathered by & glad
in my heart for such parades in tar piles
a sameness I have yearned for it's exciting
to be here fickle and demure in the hollow
to be the same a wrested thing rinsed out
& blaming yawning amid sameness
in the easy scrubland a penitent whore
settling there tho' I couldn't give a monkey's
but am beside myself again scurrying you see
as I say a sheer thing a sheer thing to torch it
& being tender among sodium plateaus

this estate glaring in white lines discarded
with rusty dogs I preach a mild amputation
some ruckus skirting the belly for sure
it's an ending forced in a precious curve
of each gormandizing town was it
just a sheer metal sheer winsome fracas
it came and went poised before slated views
a bareness of fact a puddle neutered in mud
reflecting perhaps fuelling the furze
I may stray beside the bolts & placards
beatifying the regular sort of wreckage
some cables protruding from the earth
banking on stealing a shadow in ruin
for a minute meagre on that juice
one galling entrance in the fly-tipped yard
just out of sight a tad lewd & really smashing
with a serviceable & concomitant nightguard
purging the compound in ideal takes
indolent in every instance poised shooing
blankly amid utilities & vestigial wire
caught dead to rights there yes that's it
I'd say a desert of elision a foregone thing
and plain disclosure dead again
just make your claim and then vamoose
all ongoing care and little else

Shulamith

"Scabrous and finicky as a sow," they say.
"Love's clinkers & desire's fossil!" Let's make it plain:
I've sheltered Pilgrims below my dugs
and varicose belly, it is less than courteous I'll grant you,
amid my itches, but there they all lie lodged in my gusset
in perpetuity: my boys. If I hoist my skirts you can see
them all white as sheets, a skin away from skellingtons.
I am blessed with such fine commodities to rear them
all endlessly. I scorn the ashen parvenu, investors,
chiropractors and such anatomists as I catch
scouring the ghetto's mullions, ferreting
for depilated pigs and keen pokes in the metropolis.

It is a mauvish and festering place to herd in;
there is no depression greater than that among
these turnip-eaters. Except this bunion I have perfected
is troubling this morning. Within my cloak
of orange and ochre stripes, though faded
and muddy now for sure, there are pestilential
souls banking on the demon and my kiss at their station.
It is my smell that wallops among the smeared thighs
and shingles I have fostered. Here lie the mice-men;
worm-men hemmed in amid my haunches' inky furze.
The male kind in the midst of Gallic preening,
all suckling on me now as ever. I am hardly satisfied.

I have yearned sometimes to spawn one, suck one in
to take note of the queer formulae in his spindly legs,
I would press each countenance to my breast
until the stink of me choked the vices from him
and he would be cured. It is an urge I wish to charge for.
I have never proffered my calibrated teats for free,
I own my own mind, its cavernous folds of mushrooms,
and would snap a man in two (for fear of my waters
breaking, the tantrums and shivers of the pug
skittering in blood in the cabaret of midwives)
and would rather lie coiled with my forty legions
of cats lamenting an iridescent lake of gin.

I have cordoned off a secret place behind
my sweat-filled knees, and creep there to purge
my appetites for snug pimps and braggarts.
But those lime-suckers with a stink of ocean
on their teeth, a stitch of pox, burning for a quickie,
remind me of the gurning seas, the sail-wrapped
bandits waddling down the Thames scooping
scraps of meat from wool barges. Yes, there
I'd rub my hair with tidal mud and love among
the bruised, stiffening, Ptolemaic molluscs.
Just take a stab at paradise beside those oily groynes,
though I am sick to the back teeth of tumescence.

Especially the sebaceous secretions of shining lads.
I have perfected the revenant and am prone to drunken
puking in Docklands and the Isle of Dogs. Once
I have conferred upon myself the membrane of love
I shall be a blenching multitude, the pissy dowager
herself again. It is true to say I cannot be taken.
This is my retrograde and winsome way.
I am all power in the giddy stanchions and galleria
lunching on rats and pies in the cordoned-off
erstwhile perfection of my legislature.
My elephantiasis is the new mode of god.
My strokes a defibrillating apportionment.

The Mother

i am Shulamith strung out on this march
with my boys in tow my ankles scabby i suppose
i love my womb its fragrant pith a guerdon
i make use of in featureless care at the institute
romping among actuaries & surgeons so
get me across the river for i need a hit
& understand i am more than willing
to set my boys on you though i have my doubts
my doubts with burning toes & boredom here to boot
i shall wear a mozzetta & corduroys & have my fleas
in this hefty frame enfolding some holy blokes
in all honesty the commisars i bought in a moment
of weakness chewing on rye bread just
blabbing in coffins like puritans my darlings
pale in drag & whingeing for truth & equanimity
i will oblige each with a teat in Eden & become their
headscarved double hereabouts mistress of bauxite
& barley rendering distractions on each soul
the spigot of love traipsing about for some
countermanding zealot with a cart of meat
& Distalgesics my sons up top all mischievous
the clock tower bombed again above the pigpen
& Councillors in paisley shirts spruced up
what a palaver these blokes make gesticulating
wildly when rinsing down the compound i see you
make a few quid from simnel cake and borsch
& then i'm on my way again itching & turning
across borders fetching Kalashnikovs & sour bread
for other well-hung sons i've thanked *mmm mmm*
for setting mutton under blankets for my hymns
& set beside the pavement and limewashed walls
reticulating canes stacked up like rickets below
the Ministry of Absolute Redemption a recombinant
nation beside the lampshades and soaps of the Party
Collective pure gravy under the beaks of mountains
the chipped statues of bald farts staring & staring
towards the lathered Proletariat & idling tractors
& furrows quavering to all but this seamstress
i am delivering the lord's washed out & inculcated soil

fuelling imperfect tenses in the refurbishment of race
picking over crockery & a punnet of dollars
my legerdemain swish swish upon bright perspex
cracking cement in the purges as i collect my debts
my songs impinging on crêpe banners while i point
& grin the fat lieutenants dropping loose change
in my hat indecent as a theorem as i wince impeccably
below the squirting panoply of men all verges & dogs
pert above the spittle on my lips i wipe a hanky
on the puce moon of my beautiful surviving head
above loss after loss on pillows my eructations
all smog in a city fingering tarmac for shell cases
as the trucks begin loading potash & flour sacks
the other women dissolving scurrying for haircuts
shorter than before amid the dupes & bruises
of pale concordance wishing for trains
& pronouns in the prime of this life

Lullaby

miraculous umbilical
dough emblem
a shudder
in the beset of hives
the gill infant still slick

& soufflé bone
appealingly
harmonised / toot toot
in the fecund ape
petunia agape / astir

in shunting house
or fluffer for smithies
as is all bothering
for quits in or nil on
flakes as licks in the seed

of all eyes raised ruin
having as eased an ill sense
inevitably lolling
all forage tuned
all forge in the burn ago

due to gall to pepper fuel
instead of lungs eschewing
blown mud eared
under wrinkles
& lemon rales / pancreatic

so huddled in circles still
as polish in the ridge
begins a nodule / a cell
for foam elects on spasm
in ice canker a shuck

it is sheer of some
as of old wishes / ripe to child
wishes in the wash as
stone upon stone / a care
caving in for the lip up

a reduction
leastwise veered off
in adorning blameless mud
slow perpetual sea
vermilion roost of scuds

To Tease Contrariwise

just my plainsong marionette
        limbering up old infected glass
a bleb instinct / gravity pursed before

mirrors pottering in scraps so prickly
        demurring the anabatic nude
& golgothas reticulate in offal ballast

O ash life loitering in mingy flares
        a genuflexion neat in napped lard
insouciant up alcoves & thorax a shame

it was my mix up blaring *aieeee* afar
        in soiled pairs / a burlap clump
curmudgeonly for pegs / on far tap

lame by dregs paid up or rancorous
        for a whiff suffuse of knickers / willow
paste in the kink & tin below it forming

fourways as sells for pockets in this place
        a lame course bent in by which I ham
& came & went before pent moons upsurge

gliding a goner debonair in hawking lungs
        a rasp & even chaste for referrals mown in
old spades deferred & old impacted shades

a rescued cinder godhead as true as gum
        smooth & pummelled in each boomtown tryst
& flensed once more / girt in braziers belonging

to aforementioned evenings on the boulevards
        as a routine sort for one more bypass raged
up lymphatic hugs / a lolloping mother

in some gibbon circuit ripe under fez & tulle
        a catechism censured for each province
likened to salve an old infirm adaptor

Boom Ballast

the perfectible negritude of flowers
beyond rolled temper and chiliastic tykes
an incline more spare by haste to fuel kecks
unload as careworn hides inculcate the corrugated worm

its spines to pay / unheard below kine and camps
as prudes upturn to key a hesitated bag
or loan to purge a crêpe role / a separate colour
roping in inveterate burghers to each mésalliance

a shamefaced runt keen to clone boots
& dim here to feather turks in the gazetteer
as undine in shining jaw before moisture curbs the peasants
each glee by paw done afar as the lube thickens

shell suit incurring a spinster to old camber
& belt dominion or better for zapateados
in the chichi weathered zoo as dapper for ferns
all kale in each raw trigger / a disturbed hajj

in for awhile insuring litters in a pukka litany
a petal properly tongued for potash and mimesis
protozoic fin glad for poise in each synaptic frost
or preferred gas in the dowdy rinsing glades

a duffer taking a ruddy canister all bricolage
mincing for what finials and xenon trounced in
pence and torque of hymen a poor take instead
of pelted in waspish indifferent lobes

a fleet and dismal lux imperfect in stamen
raging beyond the abattoir and smitten with pricks
hold on for galloping boulders / lyddite in the gelding pit
an august and temperate twat botched in the saga

vain in dire and wooden for drenching spores
come wave into the vetch for a daft eclectic snout afar
we lather into biscuits as pinions meet the hubbub
as donkeys count a desperate & pokey tidal bonce

Mattress Thought

ecce worm so far nigh
in meagre hugs & fair fog
a low womb vending on him
as soon as whom to whole grunts
a thicket / neuter kids far off

my runt absconding puts
on cartilage thought / a mother
blenched / elohim / erring
& come to spend packets
in a low breath / devils plump

all solace is bestowed dust
even greedy nerves in dugs
covets doubt to rub rub rub
each dog of lymph / hefty
panting for the factory mullet

remember those foiled paces
still up in the tarpaulin grind
an evanescent lung tarred so
a post for giddy liquor or blear
shanks so still as seeps so

shored up again ripe a little
all splints again piled there
a combatant joy withered
while howling gut looms pert
in bent affordable promos

& the immutable crotch stifles
one positron / the dividend
of a zygote / infecting again
each pill nerve gantry
digging down in mono flakes

flames snagged idly in winter ash
or the salve of said stages
or the salve of a fritillary
or the lame spigot & *monsieur*
bowel / each idle wash of going

Udder Music

tall glands lie mute above the fargo vein
climax on my palomino / the tracheas loafing
& ultimatum all talk / Mephisto bombed in cadre
me tearing my shift / chiffon / antonym / a sausage box
rainy in the bung light caught napping now
for a breeze greening the carer for ages *ha ha la la*

all cast in skewers & lovely abattoir a hung ratcheting
shelved in flames for the attic kilter / popes akimbo
slurry and harissa from my boys in white ties pinching it
(spent polythene crackles under the bonnet)
a veneer life as i surface rinsed to have you
veneer of / an abject fuel high-kicking for yaddo

so vexed i come as you please / a fungal atom
of sheen in a metal cage my axiom fisting for lacuna
all fur cobbles & blaring axles in the gun pump
then sobbing waves in PVC in the demi-urge pitch
i am shorn of things billing & tootling for scurf pensions
a bun gobbling nearby for a vanilla batista

just bowels faggots for insouciance & meagre skins
in the nation-weed a crux serves / a torpid loaf
all dormitory sessions / mauve / taupe envelopes
pickling the wretches (all tan & shaved) at the firm
song-bursting at Marienbad / evenings familiar
among cables / chanterelles & pogroms

i have a film shrinking in convex nubs its infirm loping
for brown coronas / rimming the virgule in hock
for another mouth canvassing what lesion & cock hankers
for leather combos i love it on opening to litigate
our ends or pulse in for wattage / creeping the rum

no means but in algae / no means but in fish
chapped for a last time in stagy pigs a bulgar slouches
no more legs in the victorious mandala / a nascent slag
of which i am *whoosh* in the gullet / palindrome-cow
for some last hatchet piece petitioned in a soft ruckus
at bottom redeemed in the leisure club

Transformer

o song i depend
for my cracks
in soul-dunking edges
end over end
a failed tank
of crisp flutes / a stank
in close habitable blush
of soot repeating

was it / a gall of tears
my beef soup lovely
in an endocrine gala
a gondola of empty hands
strolling in cheery blaze
murmuring
of tepid banks
don't make me

all haunches bare
above a flensed neighbour
basking in soot
above the treadles
of his mind
a spare song o motherland
grenade in puce
& lonely eye
above the peppered burrow

a heart-beast chomping
chopping under sweat
askance on gamine sewer
& rocking its tock
tock tock of teeth
poking all absolutes
in pimply flanks
& fiscal bedside
apparatus

old turnip face
stinking in the Volga
swishing *tra la*
my little eggs about
rollicking for the vagrant
leastwise time of yr life
& smacking of tunes
in gum thoughts & cellars

i think i am
all spade-burst vision
in a violet fist commingling
with this equitable revolution
totemic river of
the million lice
amen for that
amen amen
for spittle & for carpets

Exterminator

an acre in hand i'd say to my exterminator
attacking a madonna in this lay-by an "orgone fissure" a larval
trout bending for you "laconic tattoo" skew-whiff in some frenzy
till i reach the pistils of a complex state & bow down regardless
i love you atilla / polish me off in my snappy concrete apartment
& bulge in this city / cruising with your belly rinsed
in briny slops & cum / so worn in old ampules & sorted
citizen / erase me

house in my bowel in this simple egg my ghost wall
i am tired of shagging in the armpits of vauxhall
though my children are beset in carrying on regardless
a dusty skirt and the pinions of each fickle gear / to err
to shaft in a waste & drain from all grace under sodium artillery
a remnant grace hoity-toity with such gideon nerve as can be
as for particular care my "bulwark crimson" is indeed
a sham

modern life is so good / dripping
a stained engineer tipped for the stratagem for pallor in just lot
ecclesiastic of a kind & pukka for vacation-time / caressing
        insects
least mention of worth & the lobby heaving with the beautiful
O fuck the potent guardians wiping above my lactating frame
shilly-shallying in the wholesome chair & Wurlitzer defining
the meagre vetch
& ruin

all my marred pleasing / hormonal patina of scag / a life's rust
whirling
abject net in the fulcrum & concordance of the master pincer
passive / active / an ezekial tipped for the lime wasting gauze
in this lite perfection
solace more faecal vowing before the comely notes of an auditor
a spore of calm hanging impeccably from cerise clouds
churning the seas over Billingsgate market while giving head
i am loved in cars a wafer thin mute in the means test complex
all modest & lamenting viscera hunkered by the estate
a worm plug in the jacksie

stem of all fluid & architecture / or rampant mouth
dolorous inside burning sands
in an idling ground in out as come to / in out
over a sheer plane
a mirror / steinway shedding the lax & inarticulate floss

a chirr over the Trent lapping tidal muck and ruin
in the spinal dust trim for the leather kinship which wends its
        way
to devilry
a porpoise jeopardised in a neighbour's juice / forlorn pup
& final shard in the processions of the starchamber
loitering with their cards intact / a venal flock ashen at my tits
overcoats trim under homburgs & ideal fashion
culminating in my breeding room

& galloping perpetual

Pandemonium

leeching it had as through a small bruise penetrated
& loitered fleshy though from a separate place a yard off
all against it ends enough & parts all filthy below as jets
huzzaed over each lissom clime easing over the scarp
me parking my arse examining a groin rash moping
about or hankering after the farting heaps & chimneys
pared down from some vague hymen lifting a flap I imagine
& smatterings of the thing as we'd seen it balking
& had tuned in on perched upon it as it were from where
our programme surged in on the false salt marsh so tight
the cinquefoil of light a millenarian might chase vagrant
in fulminating as if a little bit lost I guess just stingily
pondering upon the hasp or cusp of it taking the thing
under the buckram and noting the cables tapering there
sagging under a benzene sky cannily asking for the thing
halving what the thing had caught in its teeth there
cheapened below each trauma / slurry pit / me pissing
at an approximation of it with mites of it quite free there
as though it were perspicacious for that old stepping
stone some such verdigris & moss all said a plum deal
but not least noted of in the thing taking great pains
ravening for significance through the blood sum though
not in the least disturbed but as such quailing anyhow
wandering lackadaisical under the torn fringe of ads
& virtue as I had imagined legs akimbo & channelled
the words gaping at the limpid nascent slug all bunions
& turpitude / o god I think quite pure too casting there
leavened within plastic tumblers & set with tiny stars
& tartar as such stitched booklets wd have it scratching
or so it was in the cold quarry they slept in with crab lice
under stone so pink before those tiny shits edged their gaff
those tractors rusting & the villagers boxed in in brine
blunt & lapping in the recoiled flame above a pylon
a sewer was it / perpetually tainted with music & stains
heading I would have had it towards fertile sedimentary
plateaux or the yelling of folk skedaddling at the font
those discoloured steps as I hollered in love vexed with
as far as I recollect psoriasis under the tantrum of years
& that descent in this bald time as I'd heard in the valleys

someone squatting squinting for the burlap tic-filled
paraphernalia a holding place below it no need for soft
fucks to whimper under cantilevered byres & echoes there
those steps wavering in the stairwell one more dandering
heap in those places when the thing would collapse
again as had not happened during the dry spell at all
a yard bifurcating in the den a faint twinge in my arse
my fingers footling about an inch as I probed my corpse
finally for my quim a little extravagance in the yard
in the selfsame mappa mundi all young & pure there
among the blistered whelks and fostered pandemonium

Cleaving

intervening pulse
besides a burning shower
the thing pressed no thing
pressing the need to itch
isolate one more yard
just a little fist proffered
in familiar yearning
refuge empty inchoate nights
years tipping then waning
exhilaration in my accelerator
idling gamete beyond black
my coils of forest thorns
the simple pepper of my dreams
old comfort old certainties
just a tiny panicking an oriole
or shrike confirming gorgeous waste
baking fields of sands
a flaming dust-belt
glistening with fleas
all shimmering with traffic
by underpass / overpass
twisted lazarus of each theatre
breaching boundless distance
to hate the carved hands
of the prefecture
lost in hardware a perfect
stench in cellar days
treasured bonds dwarfing
the blank interior drone
meaning resolute furnace
as tame marionettes paw over
idle over songs just that
a dividend of skin salving
as one half in thought
becomes impermanent dominion
in the bone engine
a shaft pixillated
animal again loping
beside the dilapidated infant

repealed and stripped
my numb gannet in dust
all discordant dialect
and residues of drudgery
we are alone in ash and absence
scraping up again those eyes
shaking corners / ears open
though botched with mucus /
charcoal / detergent / eau-de-cologne
wash over me now such
hinterlands beyond grey fields
one screaming tern busy
in the belly of the moment
fastened to some transient
all system and skeleton
shame-shadowed
in the pupil of the word-organ
thudding to no perfection
in the pig cells of my mouth

Ariadne

aye lofty crew scuffed in an aisle
a spur & shrill muck crooning
polished off for the foul & chaste
those years ago / spare carburettors
lumping in trysts & cauls
scant in pale hugs & poinsettia
the red ushers mitred there
hastening over lugging scallies
through a convex snare snorting

& taken for a smattering of care
prim & proper up a van to climes
dolorous for shirking crumbs
over amalgams in the lamming
game / belting on the shag pile
in ugly spores & totemic mullahs
each over scabby punnets of ash /
motet / grippe / facing off
legs akimbo shunting ajax

& his thorny firmament / cheap
for a runt / obsidian permanence
all rind endlessly sparking through
the dog shack snarling while
such fingers prick umpteen
prelates yelling fresh angles
over rum songs lapped in tar
for fulcrum silence poor prim /
prim come / come purr / relaxing

to call finally upon callow practice
tunics peeled for the populace
all tons in the stinking pot
& dancing dancing dancing
a winter eye funding sods in coma
berenice's bilious tank
of fat / in the mild room by rote
rinsing off a belly's conurbation
dreamt of & regular quartz

killed for wanting for ages here
up on the rickets & hair gel
for a stage of collocations
& stanchions / brisket / doors /
saluti alumni in your allotted dens
bedecked all miles in swaggering pips
pale infractions / tempest tunes
in my skunk city all quintessence
of purgation's kiss & err again

Quoit

done where as done can
so why of heretofore
said all in all an equal
roaming & due stale
of all said
or shipped here
half mosaic up
in the calm lax and air
preening for remembered
desiderata

a pure hankering
for aorta shed
te deum all skin
in the lake of hair
beset waif
or supine heft
for some little zone
bleakly done bleakly

blight coils
in the bitten lips
still slippy
above wicker
all ampule
in the nerve warren
where pimples on edge
veer feeling folds there
& lathering curclicues
in frost

all fingers nubs
where knotted glee
limps wide of all kin
blemished through idle ifs
& slipper dances / pent up /
all shale & a punnet
of ink retaining kippers
as singing boys fracture

the arse of it all
langsam langsam
skidding chimes
to force taxes
in the stairwell
& the ostracizing
boulevard of flame
chipper in verdure

[cut to shots of green flames
& turbid wax
& o those lovely swinging
perspex doors]

the mechanism taints
& blisters here & there
all rocketing distances

those tales
singeing over artex pistils
all vehicle now & crumbs
filling one brutish cusp
one settee fidgeting
with croup
as a squaddie furnishes
the plum spoor
coup de foudre
bending near venetian
masks legs quivering in tune
a boa draped
beside clear hosing
& rum the yellow veils
& first calls waning
in a drum of teeth

the whole puckered
as the dream bleb
guns above the whore cable
for pluck & tenure
old axioms above
the pithy frame
& kidneys set there

in an inset drain
soft as a berserker
in the slag foam
ezekial & drunken lobes
as gone before again

Melatonin

again the house fluff style
choice drift to burrow hence past
warmly elected combing combining

sweet preening of the pauper tux
look at me uttering the blown
concrete vestibule up-ended &

bestowing what idle soffits
in concatenated shelf life
a votive logos hung

like a canopy of bloody hides
the flies' tutelage
& nimble soubriquets of papaya

visors smarting in the purple
gussets of the mall
turn again each pallid frame

a system dear in dilapidated
memory a shuttle pocked
with rust where banyan trees

shimmer over cotton
horseflesh / gimlet-eyed /
so pure & barefoot in igloos of mud

i am all benign lather
in the carbon dew repository
gorse fumes in a huff / ancillary

to those deemed inviolate
as the lung fish mouthing
to inoperable glories / a tumult

heavy in crescendos of tar
a mad mix from majestic hips
& immaculate hands burst

the circle of teeth yelping
for mandalas / impetigo /
blubbing for omen in pluto's buns

i am a swarthy minx
or a glass shelter they are in
viscous in absentia or blood modes

modern implacable tartars
no grin but a man complex for it
a hovel of a thing hotelling wildly

up hymen rinsed as in a dying lamb
a man shrivels
though callow tunes siphon to

flame the wreck of him
to lie in tyres in a furrow
burning

below salt spattered headland
& always the long vales churning
towards fiscal legions

a black wolf / a bung
& rinsing dark in each shiny kiss
of one glib shank / of a thong

perpetually riven in
the dunes of language
dancing mock georgian

as the pantomime dog yields
marmalade & gingham
one cataract of horizon leering

at doldrums & pukka scenes
of avuncular nurses keen
for reeks of idle fat

bleating there
a cucumber less erudite
peering down each cinematic camber

milling for urges in the foetal bow
a dense bowel in
the marrow of the overland

& my glaucous dad
do-si-do in fungal stare or kept
in permanent gunship

the decking girl sheathed
in unremitting leisure
all blunt & dumb

Zion

torsos prim on bush & lea
the benefactors talk down the putsch
in afternoon rooms fr scag
infarctions & turbines
all commune here by which to wean
fr cauliflower & tambourines
pure legs in scrim
& full factory dancing
or another method at least
killed england: meaty england
fr barons tearing
the finger pie so waspishly

all love's a wire yard / betwixt
ship soil & needles rimmed
fr crackelure in the irwell
shelf stacking fr hinds
time owns no plastic eye nor
a gale shirking glands
o rake and rale our somnolent feasts
the leather clutch put out
& bunks & rigmarole
below scarps & kiosks
so bells deplete the dales
& the general fog abates

battalions come match yr wares
with a prisoner's coil
cheap pickings in line ups
over singlets & skelmersdale
as vehicles pop pneumatic champs
risking the waterland & mercia's glut
o where & whence the sods pout
or the ferret starts or stoat coaxes
its grimace
& jaws sag in turpentine
fr mechanized charms
& prolapse wings its weigh

each shade flummoxed
in the steak house / moping
measuring the take on hope
then there a tender glutton shaving gums
before tv approximately
shows up a donkey or ghosts
about concrete bales & quim
quizzing the jobbing droves
evens on the rats / moistened there
knocking in the oil shop
fr autochthonous rivets
yr nasdaq & yr zion

Dreck

I.

in goes each of each jongleur / dimp songs
to chuck up before a magic bendix /
for the callous ship / for wreckage
sandwiched as always hither comic eglantine
thither commune ash / on tippy toe
staring over demesnes / knackered
with alterity & guff ushering in our beds
deliberate as sand / with loaded
margins / each plangent sixty watt corridor
it is a modem extravaganza of laminates
faltering above the orthodontic blades
o rendering of all ago & climacteric whisper
lost in auxilliary podium / so tantalising
where dog lymph chunders over the immoderate
dew a shelving space plush in moulded plastic
distinguished only by the mud roster
& pitter patter of lesser beasts

2.

a mud donor in numb bemoaning egg
shattered in briny holes or fed timorous
glans / its retinue of charmers / logging
the indefinite perspex in alberta / comatose
in cheap motion & upbraided as motorhomes
mark the northerly orgone rails / distilling
patrician choirs from glorious & haggard
skies / each trinitarian salty in the motel
dressing down what spats & agents can mar
in double backs / jongleurs for pliers / & angels
laying blunt in the master copy / all's falling
in rotary club dinners / perfection milling
around spoils dropped in a phalanx of scallies
lurid in the halftone vermilion tenements
only mambo / minute by minute / a gas giant
or governing residuum boxing us in
as gorgons & intractable economies

Shulamith's Night Song

I'll drink my gallons of clouds
& wrinkle each gigantic mood
my vast electric hair   rinsing the balustrades

the shutters chatter like ants   *pink stew*
a blow torch shimmering with minstrelsy
as I dander in the ash   an umbilical chirr

uprooting stony children from metalled cambers
putting back the revolver
in the blackest moleskin bag

click   tock
its clasp indolent forceps
my lopsided groin reticulating

goading sheer heights
with a semblance of eyeballs /
milk teeth   gantries dripping like severed limbs

my bandits come   fouetté
snap   crack   a broken shin
& gelded rabbits

back in their burrows
me all perpendicular again /
strident dilapidated combination

gilded in newsprint   love sweats   iron filings
my borrowed hampered thoughts
all onion stink & chisels

filling the brigantines   *one two*
loading the mouthing pies of truth
with goitred apes

Shulamith's End Song

that old drainpipe thumping
take cover numb nuts   I'm coming for you

uh huh likened to neural fissures
my tender foes stream by   *puss puss*

to beat you up in underpass
& guildhalls   plateaux   all kinds of stuff

remaining timely husks   *violet souls*
& chickpeas in soft bowels

just giddy upstanding beasts
landing on the shelves of eyes

as though you were a new gas
in the love reek of my maidenhair

except this dirty sow didn't take it
lone snows in the ghetto   my littering now

in dandruff gethsemanes & delirium /
old mister shoe shine

when winding down / importunate rex
I'm just adjacent shadows mate / with vocal time

eager to shun mug shots
in a falling mews

I drown in automata   pattering feet
lessening the drudge work

brick & soot well up in dreams
where only just   I'll be seen in my glad rags

blemished in tar pits & spats of moss
while swifts & starlings strafe the smut

capering in that practised story /
true potting shed realism / lucifugous

with each revival song   playing rough
like a cadenza or menacing gypsy

blue tortured hands gripped
on my stash of kryptonite

& brilliantined dugs
loose in the final furlough

wiggling out of danger
& such stranger canned applause

Dream Bunions

welcome sinners
to my smiles & hugs
in mauve apologetic corridors
with foggy time in hand
borders tweezed
imperfect as a postilion
& sometimes perched
in meagre beards

above the buying traffic
one hundred tongues
as party time flies up
the anabatic routes
with shiny little fuses
or less of mortal gumption
when servicing an in-plant
skin reviving force

but mostly in tired glands
sinister as buckets
for a ribald spume or
those puce criss-crossed lips
in fuel patterns coming /
ruling cartilage
with fossil teeth
all traipsing out of town

residuum & basking
though I cannot baulk from
shucking paths & keel love
along my time dividing
plastic tendrils out from
each tidy glut
of infant fingers
pulling strings

all those wishing
drear & dreich
to lean in island rancour
poised on souls
all blessed / all blessed
in each dream gibbon
arms raised so & set
with forty lucent dolls

their little faces
glossy & quite pure
with blue injections /
or churning necks
where flying gobbets hasten
in the usual hair to lift
& care for sons or reign
among each kindled bone

Bucket Elegy

in waking moments a black brook
lopes to bleed my hair dry
through a prepared armature
and steel vague as a plantain
my wound's in-built stammering
next to the vigorous fugue objects
denying each calm future
limping past the whooshing
capillaries of each party sac

or a bouillon hugged in tape
for whom hard stains become
a colon ravening or a lower fact
raking the fracas of twenty jaws
as if we doubted there's a heaven
all shimmering transmutable
flowers piled like little attacks
on the murderous stinging inches
it is a form of gluttony

the lie of reformed plastic
a reckoning soil so chromium
the finger exercises of a lithe pupil
or a grandiose frame of storeys
predominantly reflecting tuna curves
running with that tangible lard
loving the knicker-line of mud
in the blinking musk pietàs
dumped beneath my ovum

yes it's so noticeable once woken
through a bilious cobalt winter
as starlings tip in the shrill drug
that benighted succour on pale
industrial escarpments lame again
perfect again in a momentary
gorgeous waste eternally arriving
in the quietus and sober lymph
marking each obedient drone

so it comes once a year to breakage
one myelin thread scarred as a thought
and gaudy laughs admonishing
the tidy namescapes / a furiously long
paysage milder and milder when
getting each green moment hits
preposterous metal legs and mouths
(though singed with rakish handprints)
to groan among the fissured hams

Germinator

ammonia forced down
seamlessly without gills
in a long time resurrection
just years and years
pale Judah leavened
on the bed of dollars nearby
chic and cheery miles
as each lewd bug works
established contrapuntal
charms busily beside the
mechanics of each town
holding tight those tubes
of brick and concrete
piled before the germinator
glassy esplanades dew wet
and choked with tsetse flies
or teeming bandages
hoicked-up as though
blaring and blaring
beyond each sashaying
industrial hide

most nights the same
as tears smoke and fuss
like melting prawns
on the sidewalk here
stomp stomp
budgeting for Mombasa
dragging the globe
my eggs / my eyes
scudding the fickle loci
draped with skeins
of tantrum songs
wheezing waters cold
as the veins' continuous
creaking up their
cheesy hills of light
the gin puppets picking

wrecks from needless soap
all rigid toes alone inside
electing for the choppy sink
and yearning lurid paps

Generator

its honky-tonk pistons
on the viscous tank

turning and rearing
a sodium skin

yeah yeah and seeding its signals
raiding talk of home so far awry

the piebald home / mutton love
in snotty tunes and one definite

parade before the generator
each fine Bethesda song should seem carnal

mingling with trilogies of the camp animals
to share each dowager's lips and hips

banal or asleep among
the cordoned peculiar herd

that soft lead time house
the locks all fused with knocking ice

just everything rang true
among the glottal ruins

perfection rinsing my legs
in a clay mirror

soft as a skull
whimpering for nightly gags

below the brick works
where frost strayed by one culinary tenant

farting in the commotion
bruised upon worn glissades

a crack among
cold biscuit crumbs

feeling true and voting
for headaches or the precious runt

slumped like a tiger
pouncing on one last

vestigial scar then breakfast
in our fattened land

Drum Song

commiserations friend
we've all been fixed
with bone paraphernalia
cumquats scorched in packets
decimal
voluptuous
and snide

when the talkers
call their stations
to mingle
essentially
with alien
and twisted wrecks
there can be little doubt

all of us are done
the utilities' executive
meanders by each meal
snipping fat
vociferous cables
gorging in
cold currency

and lately on bronze hills
billboards are erected
explaining that
verisimilitude
is a wasted token
and no claims
shall ever be repealed

and there beneath
the governor's pimples
nihilists propose
ten ways to wire perfection
all tantamount to heresy
as one by one
the braziers are put out

we're left the cold meat dream
of one besotted claimant
carrying a dirty great drum
(pectorals flexing)
and beating the eight-month-old
moon
in a savage cabaret tonight

which reminds us of our plastic
lewd redeemer
killing in
a damask bed
her slum collegiate
so set on rescuing
fly-by-night reps all finished up

beyond
migraines and swing
the unification
movement a fleshy
ballast needed there
to desecrate our loyal crew
and squander every bill

they're taking off
for maiming choirs
for beetle charms
for magistrates
for locust teeth
to settle down in little limbs
and hammer in each eye

Zero Start Scenario

outside the fracas
and tiny desert sit
dumb thorn fields
painted egalitarian
grey each singed
with forty thousand
vertebrae

and a mauve indefatigable
specimen yanked apart
(twisted élan)
perched over rissoles
bloating with love
trudging culs-de-sac
with crooked dolour

inside the little doors
our carbon senators'
pan-struck grins loosen
as spiralling martyrs
loiter under
cavernous block print
and mischievous beaks

come on my zeros
demons and waifs
parenting renting each
other all spasm in the
wherewithal of tired grainy
hair just scale the lessons
beyond reach

if only this outburst
frozen in a siege cage
lolling and bickering
there in an elemental
bruise of light upped
and left the sagging
creatures nearly kneeling

and all mental flames
picking fluorescent tongues
glided in numb taxonomy
raked the oven sauce
in intervals of memory
with dilapidated
amours

and all tiny vagrants
stiffened in the blast
puckered over dry
evisceration joking
like regal zeds lying
forked in the afterglow
of the devastating union band

install gut
install pins
install teeth
install egg
install tongue
install night
install beat

Notes

Poems should work in isolation and these are intended to. There is no 'official' meaning beyond that inner music of cognition we each bring to a text, but for those who wish to pursue the sources raided in these poems, here are some gleanings. No poem can be paraphrased or defined by the dissection of its subjects, and each of mine here presents a coalescing of images and language in what Paul Auster has called *The Music of Chance*.

The Gift Asphodel, Astaroth and Asmodeus are demons and appear in *Lemegeton, Clavicula Salomonis*. 1685. Sloane Collection, British Library. Cobbles are references to Dante's *Divine Comedy*.

The Levitation Eliphas Levi is a nineteenth century writer on the occult. Count Ugolino is a reference to the *Divine Comedy*. The *Theatre of Hate* is a parody of the *Theatre of Cruelty*, see Antonin Artaud. *Watch With Mother* was a popular British lunchtime children's slot on BBC television during the 1960s. *Amazing Stories* was a science fiction magazine prevalent in the 1940s and 1950s.

Hermes Lives Is an homage to Venedikt Yerofeev's masterwork *Moscow Stations* trans. Stephen Mulrine. 1997. Faber and Faber: London.

Mephisto Sleeps Is in part a reaction to the siege of Sarajevo and is informed by David Harsent's translations of Goran Simic's *Sprinting from the Graveyard*. 1997. Oxford. Louise Brooks was a major film actress in the 1930s.

The Evocation Speech of Asmoday Is a parody of a magical invocation various instances of which may be found in John Dee's (1527–1608) work, the Elizabethan occultist and Royal Astrologer to Elizabeth 1st.

Underground Is a tour of the London Underground's Northern Line. The Euminides are the Furies of Greek mythology. Fluffers is a nickname for those staff of the London Underground who clean the tracks each night. Albion is a reference to Blake's visionary poem.

The End Andreas Vesalius (1514–64) Flemish anatomist and founder of modern anatomy. Blackbird's field of souls is a reference to the sacred Serbian territory of Kosovo.

Sebastião Sebastião Salgado, photographer. The poem is a reaction to Salgado's photographs of the Serra Pelada gold mine from 1986.

Köpfe Is a dream reaction to the dismantling of civic statues of Stalin after the collapse of the Eastern Bloc and the end of the Cold War.

Mephisto Sweeps the Desert Is a dream recount of a fighter pilot in the Gulf War.

Shulamith Shulamite, the partial subject of the *Song of Solomon.*

The Mother Is a hymn to revolution. See *Mother* ("*Mat*") 1926, directed by Vsevolod Pudovkin. A mozzetta is a short cape with a hood worn by the Pope.

Boom Ballast A zapateado is a flemenco dance with rhythmic stamping of the feet. Hajj, the Muslim pilgrimage to Mecca.

Mattress Thought Takes a reference from an unpublished preface to the work of Drew Milne, to whom this poem is dedicated.

Udder Music The leisure club is a reference to Cambridge University taken from Andrew Duncan and a comment on the alleged retreat of poetry into academia.

Transform Is set in the siege of Stalingrad.

Pandemonium Refers in part to Georg Baselitz and Eugen Schonebeck's *Pandemonium Manifesto* published in 1961.

Ariadne Refers to Titian's masterpiece *Bacchus and Ariadne* 1523–24. Oil on canvas 175 x 190 cm National Gallery, London.

Melatonin Is a tempestuous survey of colonial slavery.

Zion The NASDAQ is the world's first electronic stock market.

Dreck A jongleur is an itinerant minstrel.

Shulamith's End Song Kitsch gypsy portraits in mass-produced frames were popular in British homes during the 1970s. Kryptonite is the term used to designate any surviving fragment of the exploded planet Krypton, the home world of Superman.

Drum Song Refers to the use of the Lambeg drum in Northern Ireland. Folklore has it that the Lambeg drum was brought to Ireland from Holland by troops of Duke Schomberg, William's second-in-command at the Boyne.

CHRIS EMERY was born in Oldham, Manchester in 1963. His work has appeared in numerous print and web journals including *The Animist*, *Blade*, *Conspire*, *Jacket*, *Oxford Poetry*, *Parataxis*, *Plastic*, *PN Review*, *Poetry Wales*, *Quid*, *Recursive Angel*, *The Rialto* and *Salt*. A pamphlet, *The Cutting Room*, was published by Barque in 2000. He was anthologised in *New Writing 8* (Vintage, 1999). He is Press Production Director of the Cambridge University Press and Production Manager of Salt Publishing. He lives in Great Wilbraham, England, with his wife and two children.